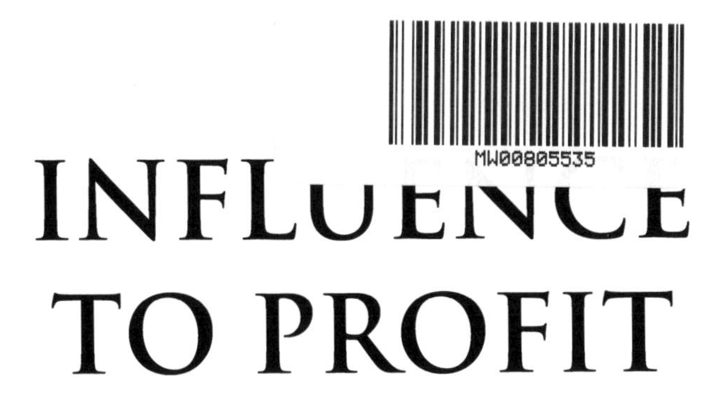

INFLUENCE TO PROFIT

TURNING WORDS INTO WEALTH WITH ETHICAL INFLUENCE AND PERSUASION

By Michael Stevenson
www.InfluenceToProfit.com

Published by Transform Destiny Publishing

Influence to Profit

Turning Words into Wealth with Ethical Influence and Persuasion

Printed in the United States of America

ISBN-13: 978-0-9963334-5-0
ISBN: 0-9963334-5-2

10 9 8 7 6 5 4 3 2 1

TABLE OF CONTENTS

FOREWORD

You're about to embark on a journey down the rabbit hole of ethical influence and persuasion. You'll learn principles in this book that people (including myself) have paid thousands of dollars for, to learn to weave words that get people to listen in both your personal and professional life.

These influence and persuasion techniques are so powerful that people in marketing, business, military and government everywhere are clamoring to get this knowledge. They are so powerful that they are even being used in most countries to win the most powerful and influential positions in government and in business and marketing to win your cash.

Practice these principles with good intentions and integrity. While these tools could be used to negatively manipulate people, once found out, people will question, shun and even completely shut out a manipulator... and that's not "influence." Real influencers focus on leadership and building relationships around win-win outcomes to maintain their influence at all times.

Once you've enjoyed finishing this book, you can take your skills to the next level and become a master of influence at our live events, listed on our website at www.InfluenceToProfit.com

INTRODUCTION

Turning Words Into Wealth with NLP

Imagine what it would be like to be one of the most powerful and skilled communicators in the world...

What would you see yourself doing? Who could you hear yourself speaking to and influencing? What would the confidence to know that you can get almost anyone to do almost anything feel like?

This is what some of the most masterful communicators on earth have experienced.

Often, some of the most unlikely people have risen to places of great power and influence, despite their looks, history or lack of education, simply because of their skill in communication.

Excellent communication has risen people to celebrity status, resolved international wars, freed people from oppression and persecution, won the highest offices in states all around the world, and created fortunes from nothing.

What can it do in your life?

Neuro-Linguistic Programming, or NLP, is a study of the subconscious mind that started back in the early 1970s. Unlike Psychology, which studies mostly disorder, NLP is a study of how the mind works to produce excellence and success, and in part, how language affects the subconscious mind in everyday conversation.

The average person thinks that subconscious mind is some deep, dark, mysterious part of the mind where we repress all kinds of dirty secrets and desires, but that old "Freudian" notion of the mind has been known to be false for decades.

In fact, your subconscious mind is just "you." It's a very powerful part of your mind which dictates all of your emotion, thoughts and actions without your conscious awareness.

Your conscious mind (the part of the mind we so love and focus on in the Western world) only makes up .006% of your mind. It is the logical, rational part of your mind. When it comes to influence and persuasion, the conscious mind is your enemy. Think of it like the guards you see in front of royal palaces. Its job is to be critical of the surrounding environment and to keep suggestions from reaching the all-important subconscious mind.

The subconscious mind is the other 99.994% of the mind. It is at the subconscious level that all decisions are made – including all buying decisions – so you can easily see that it's important to learn to communicate with it as skillfully as possible.

By using language that influences the subconscious mind, we can help lead people into states of mind that will make them more inclined to listen and to take action.

These "states of mind," or just "states" for short, are what dictate our thoughts, feelings and actions. We naturally go through the day moving from this state to that state, all the time.

If you want to influence people, you just think of what state they need to be in and then move them to it.

If you want to sell a prospect something, you need to move them from their "not interested," state, to a "buying" state.

If you want to borrow something from a friend, you need to move them from their "I'm really busy right now," state into a "doing favors" state.

If you want to get your partner "in the mood," you need to move them from their "I just want to watch TV," state, into an "I'm feeling frisky" state.

Subconscious influence is not about getting people to do things against their will. That's actually not likely, no matter how proficient you are with your language.

Rather, subconscious influence with NLP is just about using your language to easily move people from one state of mind to another. The greatest communicators, sales pros, negotiators, and yes, even seducers, all know this intuitively.

When you finish this riveting book, you'll be armed with the tools to subconsciously influence anyone, easily and effortlessly. You'll communicate effectively and resistance will melt away. The things you'll hear will leave an impression that will last a lifetime.

And once you've mastered these tools, you'll feel more confident than, perhaps, ever before. You will become an ethical influence ninja!

PART ONE

Turning Words Into Wealth

CHAPTER ZERO

The Ethical Part of Ethical Influence and Persuasion

This topic is so important that it even comes before Chapter One.

When I speak around the world on the topic of influence and persuasion – especially influence of the subconscious mind – this question always comes up…

"Isn't this all just manipulation?"

That's a very common question when it comes to influence and one we should address right away.

Let's look at the definition of the word:

ma·nip·u·late tr.v.
To move ... especially in a *skillful* manner

The fact is, all communication is manipulative. All words we speak affect people and influence people's thoughts by moving them from thinking about one thing to another.

The part the most people lack is the "skillful" part.

The thing most people are concerned with when they bring up the "manipulation" word has nothing to do with the *tools* of communication, but rather the *intention* of the person communicating.

A spoon can be used to feed a baby at home, or kill a man in prison. The spoon itself is neither good nor bad, it's just a tool. It's the intention and action of the person using the tool which determines the motive.

The same is true for the tools in this book.

Could these skills be used in a win-lose, "manipulative" sort of fashion? Of course... all language can do that. You don't even need influence skills to manipulate people.

While these skills could be used in a deceptive, win-lose manner, that behavior will ultimately lose influence over time resulting in less influence.

Using these skills for win-lose purposes will hurt people and damage relationships, and that's not influence. When people distrust you and stop listening that's the opposite of influence.

Novice influencers are always trying to force

people to do something they want, which is why they only get results with those who are already easily manipulated, often burning their victims to the point of destroying relationships.

An ethical influencer takes no pride in this kind of manipulation. The skills I'm going to share with you in this book contain neither coercion, deception nor manipulation. Rather, they are about creating authentic relationships and win-win situations where people *want* to do what you're asking.

The techniques you'll learn in this book influence people. They do not control people.

As a matter of fact, NO form of influence or persuasion techniques will ever control others (regardless of what other authors promise in their marketing), but it does allow you to find greater success in communication by **bypassing the most critical part of the**

mind and **speaking to the most powerful part**: the subconscious mind.

The communication skills you'll learn and master in this book are designed to augment who you authentically are and to communicate your message more clearly to create win-win outcomes.

When used skillfully with pure win-win intentions, these influence and persuasion techniques create relationships that will continue to produce fruitful results for you and everyone involved.

CHAPTER ONE

THE GATEWAY TO THE MIND

The key to influence lies in understanding the subconscious mind – the other part of your mind that is out of your awareness – which represents about 99.994% of the mind.

The subconscious is the part of you that runs your body, protects you from harm, manages your memories, stores your beliefs and values, runs your habits and generates your emotions.

When it comes to influence, it's important to remember that people don't make decisions logically – we make them emotionally. When President Barak Obama used subconscious influence language patterns to win the

Presidential election, he didn't make a logical case for his presidency, like his competitors. He brought people to tears and moved them to vote by tapping into their emotions.

The subconscious mind does not think in words like your conscious mind does... It thinks in pictures, sounds and feelings.

Think of your last good daydream. As you sat there in your chair, perhaps staring at one spot or another, your eyes defocused, your facial muscles relaxed, and all the sounds of the day just faded away as you lost yourself in the internal world of the subconscious mind.

As this happens, that chatter that usually exists inside your mind disappears. Your subconscious mind takes over as the words disappear, and you get lost in the imagination.

To unlock the gateway to the mind and

influence others subconsciously, you must learn to tap into this emotional conduit by creating pictures, sounds and feelings in people's minds that move them.

Using sensory-based language that engages people's imagination and emotions is one of the most powerful influence tools available. It's often said that if you want a person to do something for you, take them there in their mind, first.

When I want to convince someone to come to one of my live trainings, for example, I use language like the following:

"Bill, when you come to this training and see the material I'm teaching, I know you'll be as excited as I was when I first learned it. You'll connect with people just like you who also have a burning desire to be heard, to give yourself a voice, and to learn to influence others with integrity.

"Imagine hearing yourself speaking to others in a way that's powerful, confident, and influential, and how it makes you feel to see yourself finally achieving all those things you want in life. When you think about it that way, I know you can see all the reasons why this sounds like a great idea, doesn't it?"

Notice how I'm using visual words (see, imagine), auditory words (heard, voice, hearing, sounds), and feeling words (excited, connect, burning, powerful, confident, feel).

These kinds of words engage the listener, cause them to "go inside" to create that experience, and, ultimately, move them into a "state" of your design.

There is one important thing to point out. Since the Subconscious mind thinks in pictures, sounds and feelings, it has a very hard time processing negatives. Negatives are virtually impossible to represent using pictures, sounds and feelings.

You just can't not think about something without thinking about it first. If I say, "don't think of a black cat," what are you thinking about right now? A black cat! It's as if the subconscious mind simply erases words like no, not, don't, can't, shouldn't, never and other negative words.

This is one of the biggest mistakes I hear novice influencers make. They create the wrong state by using negatives in their language.

Anyone who has ever had children has seen this play out. When you tell your child, "don't spill your milk," the child will immediately make a picture of spilling the milk in their mind – they must do this, just to even understand the words. This picture created by the "embedded command" to spill the milk will put the child into a "clumsy state," and they will reach right out and spill the milk!

If you tell someone not to eat the cookies in the kitchen, they say, "Cookies?! Where?!" You've moved them into a "hungry state," just by mentioning them.

Think of the body like a robot that simply responds to the pictures, sounds and feelings in the mind.

Many novice influencers try to begin with statements like these:

"You probably won't want to do this..."

"I'm sure you're not interested..."

"Now, don't be offended..."

"Don't be alarmed..."

"This isn't what you think it is..."

While these statements might seem to be influential to the *average* influencer, you, becoming a subconscious influencer, now know that negative statements like these will absolutely destroy your chances of influencing people.

Get Your FREE **Influence to Proft Resource Kit** with more great examples, influence scripts, bonuses, and videos at:

www.InfluenceToProfit.com/book-resource-kit

CHAPTER TWO

PACING AND LEADING

Wouldn't it be great if you could make someone listen to you? Even the greatest of influencers can't force people to do what they don't want to do, but what if you had a way to keep people listening and keep them open and receptive to your ideas, no matter what?

To lead a person into the state you want, you must begin by speaking to the state they're currently in by using language that matches this state. This is called, "pacing," a person's current state.

Once you have paced the person's state, you have engaged the subconscious mind to pay attention, and now you can lead them into another state. Without first pacing the subject's state, you have no hope of leading them into your desired state.

Imagine that you're having a great day, but one of your co-workers is grumpy. What do you think will happen if you wave at them and say, "Hey, it's a FANTASTIC day today, isn't it?!"

Because you're conflicting with their state, you would lose all of your power to influence. They will probably sneer at you and maybe even avoid you all day long!

If you've ever been in a conversation with someone who disagrees with you, then you know the feeling that comes up when someone "mismatches" your state. You get defensive, you dig your proverbial feet in, and communication shuts down as you become determined to prove your point over theirs.

This is what most amateurs do. They are thinking only in terms of what they want – standing at the "finish line" – and trying to get the other person at the "starting line" to come to them.

To be an expert influencer, you have to learn to meet people where they are and lead people into the desired state gracefully.

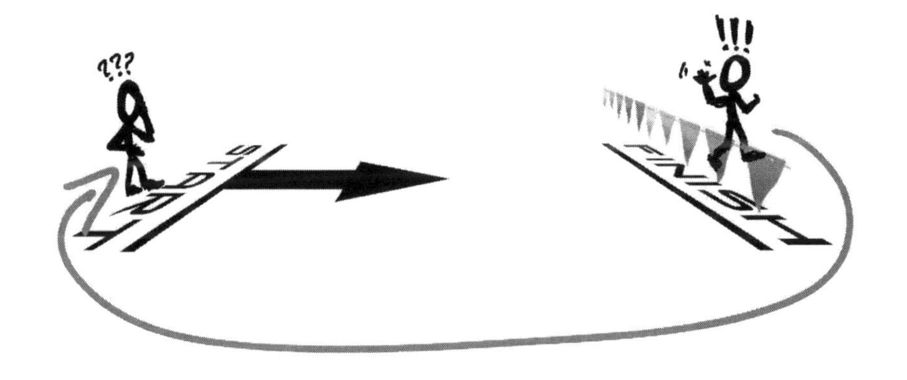

If the person says, "I'm really angry with you right now!" don't say, "You're overreacting," or, "That's ridiculous!" That will only clash with their current state and make them angrier!

Even if you get defensive and say, "Hey, I didn't do anything wrong!" you're going to mismatch their state and you'll lose all hope of leading them out of it.

Instead, learn to match or respect their state. Consider the following response:

"I can see that you're really angry, and you have a right to be! I would be angry to, if I felt someone had done that to me!"

Said with the same body language and the same intensity of voice while respecting the state that they're in will immediately begin to diffuse the situation. The best part is, you haven't admitted any wrongdoing or assumed any blame. You've only acknowledged their right to be angry based on their current understanding of the situation (which may or may not be accurate).

Once you've matched their state, then you can begin to lead them out of it, subtly, little by little. Here's another, more detailed example:

Client: "I'm so pissed off that you screwed my order up, I'm <u>never</u> going to do business with you people again!"

Influencer: "You *are* really pissed off, and you have a right to be! I would be angry to, if I felt someone had done that to me! And the first thing I would do is yell and scream at the person. As a matter of fact, <u>I'm</u> pretty pissed off that we haven't made you feel taken care of. I'm going to see what I can do right now to fix this situation for you. If I can do that right now, you'd be willing to think about keeping your account with us, wouldn't you?"

As you can see, this exchange would totally take the wind out of the client's sales. It would be virtually impossible for this client to continue their tirade after pulling out these ethical influence skills.

If you were in a sales situation and your prospect said, "I'm not sold on this," you wouldn't reply with, "What? Not sold?! This is the best product in the field!" That would surely break rapport!

Instead, pace and lead them to the buying state. "That's right, you're not sold yet. That's because you haven't asked the one question that will have you totally and completely sold right now. So what's on your mind?"

When the prospect issues a statement like, "I'm not sold," they're putting the ball back in your court with a challenge. By responding with an influence pattern like the one above, you are skillfully putting the ball back in their court with some verbal aikido (the martial art where you use your opponent's momentum against them).

Pacing and leading is a powerful influence and persuasion skill in your arsenal that will improve every other principle in this book and all your communication in general. Practice it well and you'll become more influential almost immediately.

Get Your FREE **Influence to Proft Resource Kit** with more great examples, influence scripts, bonuses, and videos at:

www.InfluenceToProfit.com/book-resource-kit

CHAPTER THREE

Cause and Effect

Master influencers know that linking their suggestions to other "known" things makes people more likely to accept the suggestions. This next principle is a perfect example of that.

Cause and Effect is a language pattern linking one thing to another. We say things like this naturally all the time:

"The earthquake caused the picture to fall off the wall."

"If you stick your finger in a power socket then you'll get shocked."

"It's cold in here because the door is open."

"Since you're late, we're going to miss the movie."

In all of these statements, it's clear that one thing causes, or caused, another thing.

The human mind thinks in Cause and Effect, so when we hear Cause and Effect statements like these, as long as the cause is plausible then we tend to accept the effect part of the statement without question, and vice versa.

This is where the Cause and Effect principle becomes so powerful as an influence pattern.

Cause and Effect statements take the following forms:

"X makes you Y."

"If X, then Y." (Note: the word "then" may be

left out)

"Since X, then Y." (Note: the word "then" may be left out)

"As X, then Y." (Note: the word "then" may be left out)

"Y because X," or "Because X, Y."

Or any other language that assumes one thing caused another.

By using these patterns to link something you want the person to think to something that's already true, it makes people likely to accept what you're saying.

Here are some examples of using these statements persuasively:

"Reading this page makes you **want to devour the rest of the book**."

"If you use this one technique, then you'll **want to tell all your friends**."

"Since you're reading these words, you're **becoming better at influence**."

"As you influence more people, you'll **want to tell them about this book**."

"**You'll want to buy my influence books and courses**, because people are secretly using these persuasion tricks on you."

In each example above, I'm linking a truism (usually, the Cause) to a suggestion I want you to accept (usually, the Effect side of the sentence, the bold words), making it more likely I will influence you to do those things.

Notice that the Cause and Effect relationship does not have to be true. It only has to sound plausible enough for them to accept the suggestion.

This is a powerful tool in your influence arsenal, and the more you use it, the more you'll want to discover.

CHAPTER FOUR

Yes Sets And The Hypnotic Nod

You're reading this book, absorbing these words, and learning how to become an Ethical Influencer, and that means you'll want to learn more from me, doesn't it?

We humans are very repetitive creatures, and when we get into a repetitive routine, we tend to follow it without question.

Enter the "Yes Set."

The Yes Set influences a person to agree with you, almost out of sheer repetitiveness. This influences a part of the brain called Broca, which detects patterns. When it detects a pattern, it shuts down critical thinking by the brain for efficiency.

When using a "Yes Set," the idea is to say several things in a row, which the other person will definitely say, "Yes" to each of those things.

For example, I opened this tip with several statements. "You're reading this book (yes), absorbing these words (yes) and learning how to become an Ethical Influencer (yes)..." Each of these is undeniable.

Once the pattern is set, I follow-up these yeses with the suggestion I want you to accept and believe: "... and that means, you'll want to learn more from me (yes!)..."

The key to Yes Sets is to base them off of observations to which the subject will undeniably say, "Yes." But beware: the moment you mismatch them and say something questionable, your subconscious influence is lost. So be sure to make each statement undeniable.

There are two keys to this. First, avoid statements that have too much detail. The more detail you offer, the more there is to disagree with, so the less detail the better. You can sometimes get away with saying things that are so ambiguous they don't really mean anything at all, yet they're still true.

For instance, "There you are, doing what you're doing, and you're doing it for a reason which you may or may not know, and that means you'll eagerly read the rest of this book just before you recommend it to everyone."

The second key is the Hypnotic Nod, one of the subtlest yet most powerful hypnotic influence tools.

As you say each statement in the Yes Set, lock eyes with your subject and begin nodding your head. Start very subtly, and build up the nod towards the end into a full head nod. You'll find that your subject will begin nodding with you, even if they don't want to – it's that powerful!

CHAPTER FIVE

HYPNOTIC ASSUMPTIONS

Another hypnotic influence skill is the art of hypnotic assumptions, called "presuppositions." To presuppose simply means to assume something without really saying it.

One classic presupposition was used in retail sales for years. Most sales people were trained to never ask, "Do you want to buy that?" because the answer might be "Yes" or "No." Instead, they would walk up as you were holding a product and ask, "Will that be cash or check?"

The purchase is assumed by the second question. It's a "yes," or "yes," question, instead of a, "yes," or "no," question. This causes you to make pictures, sounds and feelings in your head of buying the product, which you're now more likely to do.

I used a presupposition in the beginning of this book when I said, "When you finish this riveting book, you'll be armed…" Notice that by using the word, "when," I am *assuming* that you will do what I want you to do (finish the book).

Here's another example. If I wanted you to think this book has incredibly influential language patterns in it, I wouldn't just say, "This book has incredibly influential language patterns," because you might choose to second-guess or doubt my statement. It's just too direct.

I could presuppose the same thing like this: "Have you seen the incredibly influential language patterns in this book yet?"

This presupposition shifts the focus of the statement off of the suggestion (incredibly influential language patterns) to whether you've seen them or not. You have to *assume* the book has these incredibly influential language patterns to answer the question of whether you've seen them or not.

There's a second presupposition in the word, "yet," which assumes that you will eventually see them — it's only a matter of time!

Presuppositions often use what we call, "positive, suggestive language." But the most amazing thing about them is that they don't *have* to use positive!

I could get you to assume the same suggestion by saying, "You haven't seen the incredibly influential language patterns in this book yet." Even though it's a negative statement, you still have to assume and accept the same suggestion! This is sneaky ninja stuff!

Here are some examples of using presuppositions:

"Joe, you're going to find yourself excited once you get my product into your home." (Assumes the product will get into his home)

"How many ways do you know that this book has benefitted you?" (Assumes the book has benefitted him, the only question is how many ways)

"Should I pick you up Friday night or Saturday night?" (A yes or yes question; Assumes you will pick them up)

"There are five reasons you'll want to finish this book and one of them is because you enjoy it so much." (Assumes there are several good reasons, even though you only give them one

— very powerful!)

"When you think of the ways you can use my product, buying it now is an easy decision, isn't it?" (Assumes the prospect has ways of using it they may not be consciously thinking of, yet)

Using language like this allows you to "assume the sale," which will have people listening to you and following your suggestions like an influence master.

CHAPTER SIX

INFLUENCE IS IN YOUR FUTURE

Six months from now, you'll look back on this book as one of the best books you've ever enjoyed, because the benefits you've gotten from ethically influencing people were so good for you. I'll bet you already want to tell everyone to buy it because you enjoyed it so much.

While the conscious mind is a mind of, "now," at the subconscious level, past, present and future all exist simultaneously.

This means, often, you will need to persuade the other person's "future self," (and, sometimes even their "past self!") to say yes, too.

Not only does your subconscious mind store all the memories of your past, but it also stores "future memories."

For example, think about what you're doing next Saturday. There's already a picture or a concept of next Saturday in your mind, isn't there? Think about what you'll be doing in one month, six months, a year. Your subconscious has a notion of those things, too.

Your subconscious mind is continually moving in the direction of a future that it has already devised inside your mind. The same thing is true for people you are influencing. So, if the thing you're trying to get them to do is in conflict with that future, you will have a hard time persuading them. You want use your words to build a new future for the person to move towards.

To influence someone to do something such as make a purchase, help them build that future in their mind. This is called "Future Pacing."

Don't just take them to the moment of purchase – take them beyond it, where the outcome is a certainty because it has already happened in their mind.

For example, one of the ways I help people make the decision to attend my live workshops is like this:

"Joe, imagine that you've attended my workshop and six months has passed since you graduated the course. You've spent several months using these techniques, seeing the results, hearing others praise you and feeling confident. Looking back on the training, what was the most important thing you got out of it?"

This language locks in the notion that they will come to my training and will get immense benefit from attending, all without directly telling him to come. This presupposes that Joe will attend the workshop by talking about the benefits he receives afterwards, for as much as six months.

Here are some examples of using Future Pacing in everyday conversation:

"Amy, how good will you feel a year from now, knowing that it was this security system that has been keeping your family safe, secure and worry-free?"

"You're going to look back on this day as one of the most satisfying decisions you've ever made."

Sometimes you will even want to speak to the person's past to get a yes:

"In the future, when you think about how it used to be in the past, before you took this product home, you'll probably chuckle at how easy it is now, after all those years of struggle became just a distant memory."

"What would the 'future you' tell the 'past you' so you can feel good about taking this product home with you today?"

CHAPTER SEVEN

Double Binds

When it comes to influencing others, it's important to remember that nobody likes to be manipulated against their will. People always want to feel as if they have a choice in the matter.

Novice influencers are always trying to force their subjects to do something, which is why they only get results with those who are already easily manipulated.

When people feel as if they have no choice, they will resist your influence at nearly all cost, so the way to keep people open to your suggestions is to always offer choice — even if it's only the *illusion* of choice. This is the power of the double bind.

When my son was a young boy, his bedtime was 9:00 PM. Some nights — especially the nights where he was acting hyper — I would want him to go to bed early, so I would offer him a choice. I would say, "Jonathan, I'm going to let you watch your favorite show on the TV. Once it's over, do you want to go to bed at 8:45 or at a quarter-to-nine?"

He would always say, enthusiastically, "Quarter to nine, Dad!" Of course, to his young mind, a quarter-to-nine sounded later, even though it's the same exact time as 8:45!

The purpose of the double bind is to give people the illusion of choice, so they feel as if they have options, even though both options actually result in the same exact outcome. In sales, this is often called the "Alternative Advance Close."

The trick is to think of what you want the person to do and then come up with two ways for them to do it. Those two ways become your double bind.

For example, if I want someone to purchase my book, I might say, "Joe, which would you rather go home with today, the paperback or the hardback?" Notice, I'm not offering the prospect the choice of "No thanks, I'm not interested." The double bind is about choosing one or the other. In either case, both choices result in the same thing — a sale for me. This is an example of a "yes or yes" presupposition.

When my son was a boy, he won the Cub Scout fundraising competition by using a double bind. Most of the other kids were asking, "Do you want to buy a candy bar?" (a yes or no question) My son asked people if they would like to buy "five candy bars, or two?" (a yes or yes question) He sold two candy bars at almost every house, and even sold five at a few houses.

Double binds are to be used subtly and gently. If you're mowing people down with double binds left and right you're likely to get a reputation as a verbal bully, so use them with care, or you can just choose to be careful how you use them. It's totally up to you.

CHAPTER EIGHT

THE ART OF THE NEVER-ENDING QUOTE

Quoting another source — especially a source of authority — is a highly persuasive way of influence because people tend to be naturally influenced by those of high prestige and authority.

But when you're quoting a person who is not in the vicinity to defend the statement, it becomes very difficult to argue against it.

For instance, if I told you, "I'm afraid of aliens coming in UFOs pillaging our planet and killing all human beings so they can have earth to themselves," you may think I'm completely nuts and you might even tell me so!

But what if I tell you that renowned quantum physicist Stephen Hawking, one of the most brilliant and knowledgeable people on the subject of space, is certain of alien life and thinks we should fear them? He said, "I imagine they might exist in massive ships, having used up all the resources from their home planet. Such advanced aliens would perhaps become nomads, looking to conquer and colonize whatever planets they can reach." (By the way, that's a real quote)

Well, now, that becomes a little harder to argue with, now doesn't it?

Now, imagine if I said to you, "The other day, I was talking to my brother-in-law, who's boss told him the most interesting thing that he read in an article in TIME Magazine, where Stephen Hawking said, 'I imagine they might exist in massive ships, having used up all the resources from their home planet. Such advanced aliens would perhaps become nomads, looking to conquer and colonize whatever planets they can reach.'"

This is what is called an extended quote. In it, I quote my brother in law, who quotes his boss, who quotes TIME Magazine, who quotes Stephen Hawking.

At this point, two things happen. First, it becomes virtually impossible to argue against the point. The listener just ends up accepting the final premise. Second, it becomes so hard for the listener to keep track of who said what to whom, that they actually produce an overload of the conscious mind and they become *even more* influenceable.

The other day, I was talking to this woman, Susan, whose husband came to one of my NLP trainings, and he told her about this guy Greg in the class who was getting instructions from another student who told him that this is one of the easiest ways to get people to accept your suggestions.

Of course, as with most things, there is a point of diminishing returns. You can only extend the quote out to about eight to twelve people before your listener will get confused, get annoyed and tune out.

CHAPTER NINE

Being Artfully Vague

As you think about all those ways that you know how to communicate, you know that, often, some people have that certain ability to captivate the attention of everyone. That realization you have, as you hear this thing or that thing they say, makes you feel something, doesn't it? Because you know that they know how artfully vague they are when they do it, right?

Did the above paragraph make your head spin a little? You may have noticed that, while there are many words, it really didn't say much at all. That's because it is "artfully vague."

Renowned psychiatrist and hypnotherapist,

Milton H. Erickson, was well known for this kind of speech, because he created a hypnotic style based on it called "Conversational Hypnosis."

Imagine that inside your mind is a search engine, just like the one you would use on the internet. If I say "moon," your mind does a quick look-up, and probably only one result comes up — the Earth's moon, Luna.

But if I say "flower," your subconscious has to do a little more work. There are more things that are "flower," than just one. However, even this is a quick search, because you'll likely come up with a picture or memory of your favorite flower as your first result.

Flower is a word that's vaguer, so the subconscious mind has to contemplate it to understand it.

Now, if I say, "Remembering all those thoughts you were thinking yesterday... yes, *those* thoughts," I've gotten even more vague. That's not even something your conscious mind can hold in your awareness, which is limited in capacity, compared to your subconscious mind.

Your subconscious mind has to do the search and then shuffle through thousands of results, trying to find out which meaning to deliver to your conscious mind as a thought.

During this subconscious search process, which Milton Erickson called a *transderivational search,* you actually enter a light "trance state," and your conscious mind's ability to reason, analyze, think logically, and (most importantly) reject suggestions, is greatly diminished.

This is a process which is increasingly being used in two fields which are getting better and better at manipulating people subconsciously:

marketing and politics.

In several studies, it has been shown that political candidates in the US were using as much as 58% hypnotic language patterns in their speeches.

There are several ways that you can use this kind of ambiguous speech (called *ambiguities*) to keep a person in a light trance and make them more persuadable.

Universal Statements

A universal statement is anything you say that includes either everything or nothing. For example, if I say "Thinking of all of your thoughts," it's universal because of the word "all." In other words, it's not referring to a specific thought, which makes the mind go into a "trance state" to search the thought I'm referring to.

The following sentence is loaded with universals, "Using universals always makes people persuadable in every situation, all the time, and never does nothing."

A popular marketing slogan that uses Universals is from Adidas: Adidas is All In

The following words are universal in nature: all, none, everything, nothing, always, never, everybody, nobody, total, complete.

The following are examples of Universal statements:

- Nobody has this kind of service.
- We represent everything you know about quality.
- Service is Everything
- Everyone knows this is true.
- Nothing is better than this.

Frozen Actions

Frozen actions happen when you turn a verb (an action word) into a noun (a person, place or thing word). For example, if I say, "We have a lot of communication here," it sounds as if "communication" is a thing — but it's not!

Communication is not something you can have (like a thing). It's something you do (action). By referring to it as a "thing," it's as if we are freezing it in time.

Communication involves the act of "communicating," which involves many steps, and happens over time. By turning it into a "thing," we confuse the mind, because it can't actually make a picture, sound or feeling of the thing, which are the primary ways in which the mind thinks and understands.

The way to test if a word is a Frozen Action is

by asking yourself, "Can I put this in a wheelbarrow?" If the answer is yes, it's a thing. If the answer is no it's a frozen action.

If you've ever been to a business conference, filled with corporate buzzwords (which are usually Frozen Actions), you know how mind-numbing these can be. Your mind starts to wander off to a distant place, because the words you're hearing should have meaning, but it's too hard to figure out. Your conscious mind finally surrenders, and "trance" occurs.

This is why it is sometimes so hard to read "white papers" and other technical documents.

The following are examples of words which are Frozen Verbs with their verb counterparts: thoughts (think), feelings (feel), emotions (emote), cares (care), worries (worry), fears (fear), hesitation (hesitate), anticipation (anticipate), enjoyment (enjoy), fulfillment (fulfill).

Often, you can turn an action word into a Frozen Action by adding the letter "-s," the letters "-tion," or the letters "-ment" to the end of the action verb.

Ambiguous Actions

Ambiguous actions are action words that don't tell you how to do the action. If I tell you to reject the politics of the world, what does that mean? Does that mean to dislike them, to ignore them, to protest against them, or something else?

There's no information in the word "reject" that tells you how to do it, so the subconscious mind has to go inside, scan the internal search results, and try to come up with an action that matches.

These words can be very influential when used properly. Here are a few Ambiguous Action words: try, do, fiddle, subdue, maneuver, manipulate, control.

Ambiguous Subjects

If you remember back to elementary school grammar, every sentence is supposed to have a *subject* — a word which specifies the person, place or thing you're talking about.

Of course, we Ethical Influencers leave out specifics when we're being ambiguous. Using the Ambiguous Subject means that you leave out or confuse whom or what you're talking about.

For example, if I say, "They really like to use subconscious influence language," who am I talking about? The word "they," is ambiguous.

"People can use this language pattern," (which people?). "Because they are very good," (they, meaning the people, or they, meaning the language patterns?). "When one masters this pattern," (one who?). "The people will be influenced," (which ones?).

Some Ambiguous Subject words are: they, them, it, those, people, one, many, some, anybody, anyone, someone

One-Sided Comparisons

One-Sided Comparisons are easier. They tend to work better. It's because they're more ambiguous. They have a greater capacity for trance, because they're quicker.

You may notice in the four sentences above, that something important is left out. In each sentence, there's a comparison being made — easier, better, more, greater, quicker. But what am I comparing to?

In each of the sentences, the item I'm comparing to is left out, so the comparison is one-sided. In other words, instead of saying, "They tend to work better than a stick in your eye," which would be comparing one thing to another, it's just, "They tend to work better."

This does two things. First, it causes the person to go "inside" to try to figure out what the comparison is. Second, it makes the suggestion *easier* to accept (did you catch that word, "easier"?).

For example, if I said to you, "You should buy this new car. It's more affordable than a cup of coffee," you would laugh me off the lot! The comparison is obviously bogus!

But, if I instead said, "You should buy this new car. It's definitely more affordable," then my suggestion that the car is affordable is more easily accepted.

This is a highly influential method of communication, but remember, it's *better* to leave the comparison one-sided.

One-sided comparison words are: better, worse, more, less, easier, harder, brighter, dimmer, heavier, lighter, cheaper, pricier.

You can use virtually any normal comparison word, just remember to leave off the thing you're comparing to.

Here are some examples:

"We have always given better service."

"Our product is more reliable."

"This is a better choice."

"We're Avis. We're #2, so we try harder." (A real-world example)

CHAPTER TEN

HYPNOTIC STORIES AND METAPHORS

By far, the most influential form of communication is metaphor. Metaphors are influential stories that lead a person into the state you desire.

I once trained a student named Todd who, after learning some of my influence language patterns went home to Arizona.

He tried explaining these things to his wife, telling her about all the things he learned, but she simply wasn't getting it. He said, "Honey, if you *learn to use these patterns*, everything is possible. A person can have anything they want. They can have love, happiness, contentment, profit... anything at all."

His wife had been telling her best friend about all the things that Todd had told her that I said about subconscious influence being the most effective ways of communicating, but she was skeptical.

He said, "Really honey, this way of communicating is better and I can prove it! All you have to do is *use it.* Just try one little language pattern each day, and they'll start to *become habit.*"

She said, "Fine, you can make me *believe in subconscious influence,* if you accept a challenge from me. If I find that *it's better than normal language*, I'll believe you and I'll start to *use it everyday.*"

That day, they were walking along the street, admiring the nature on their walk. They could see the colors of nature dancing and swaying in the wind. They could hear the melodic tweeting of the birds and feel the warm sun beating down on their faces.

Then she challenged him. She said, "When we get to the coffee shop, you work your magic, and if you can get a cup of coffee for free, I'll *be convinced.*"

At the coffee shop, after his wife ordered a tea, he began having a conversation with the barista by meeting her in her state...

He said, "It seems like you're working hard."

She replied, "Yeah! But I like my job."

He said, "That's better, isn't it? To have that special thing that you love. That makes it the most enjoyable thing in the world, but I'll bet it's not as enjoyable as that vacation you went on."

She lit up said, "No! How did you know about that?"

He continued, "Isn't it nice to know that as you think about that now, the memory of it makes you feel wonderful? It kind of breaks you out of your work and makes you feel better, doesn't it? It's nice when you can *give someone a gift* like that, isn't it? *Like me*... I really do love to go on vacation. Where I can *be free* to just do something that makes me feel good, just because *you want to*, ya know?"

At that point, she smiled, blushed a little, cocked her head and said, "Hey, would you like a cup of coffee while you're waiting? It's on the house."

His wife almost dropped her tea!

As you look back over that story, you may notice several things, but first, I'll tell you my intention for the story.

Of course, the overt purpose of the story is to tell you something interesting, or entertaining; something that will keep your conscious attention.

But my covert purpose was to "install" in you the idea to practice this every day, and the belief that hypnotic influence works.

This is, by the way, a true story from one of my graduates, Todd in Arizona.

Influence metaphors don't have to be true, but telling true stories helps to keep track of the details. Plus, the stories that are personal to you are the one's you'll be able to associate to ("get into") the most.

Of course, the story contains many of the hypnotic influence patterns that you've learned, throughout this book. There was also extended use of quotes to help you accept my suggestions that are built into the story.

There's one other great tidbit in these stories, called "Embedded Commands." These are words which are somehow distinguished from the other words of the story. In writing, they're often italicized, bolded or underlined. In speaking, they're often said with a lower tone of voice, or a slower speed.

Your subconscious mind is very good at noticing these differences, but your conscious mind usually misses them. So, the suggestions go directly into the subconscious.

Go back over the story and look for them. They're there!

These suggestions can be embedded in almost any communication — even if it has nothing to do with the command!

The founders of NLP used to tell a story that started with, “Remember when Mom used to bake cookies from *scratch*? *Your* mom used to do that, right? Everybody *knows* what that’s like,” and within minutes, the whole audience was scratching and rubbing their nose, because the command “scratch, your, knows (nose)” was subtly emphasized in the sentence!

Practice these embedded commands and get to the point where you can speak them in a lower tone of voice or slower speed, subtly, so the conscious mind doesn’t catch on. Your suggestions will go directly into the subconscious mind.

CHAPTER ELEVEN

THE POWER OF A CROWD: SOCIAL PROOF

As evolved as the mind is, a built-in subconscious "program" can be used to your advantage when influencing the masses. This program is what I call, efficiency of thought.

Economy of thought states that the subconscious mind will always take the path of least resistance. If given two choices – A) come to the right conclusion yourself, or B) infer the correct conclusion by using other, pre-existing clues – the subconscious mind will usually pick option "B."

While option "A" might allow you to rationally

weigh your options, carefully thinking through each of the variables to give you the best outcome, this takes time. Option "B" allows the subconscious mind to save time and energy.

Social proof is one of these cases where the mind chooses option "B."

Social proof is the pattern of thought that says, "If everyone else is doing it, so should I." The rationale of the subconscious mind is that if other people are doing it, they must have carefully thought out the options and come to the right conclusion, so I can trust the "crowd."

While this isn't always true, it is the default behavior of the subconscious mind.

This is a ploy often used by restaurant, bar and club consultants that you've probably been a victim of, yourself. One restaurant I know of opens for dinner at 5:00 PM sharp. But even if you have a 5:00 PM reservation, it's likely you won't be seated until 5:30 PM to 5:40 PM. The restaurant is open, music is playing, tables are set and the wait staff is present, yet they ask you to stand by in their outside waiting area. The "line" outside continued into the night.

The result? The restaurant quickly became the talk of the town. People said things like, "It must be good... look at how busy they are!"

Clubs in places like Hollywood and New York City will often have a line outside, even if the inside of the club is empty. This helps to promote the, "popular and exclusive," public appearance they know will boost business.

P.T. Barnum once said, "Nothing draws a crowd like a crowd."

While the principle of social proof hasn't changed a bit since old P.T. Barnum's circus days, the way we convey social proof has changed dramatically.

As Seth Godin says in the book, "Unleashing the Idea Virus," media such as the Internet has created a megaphone and placed it in the hands of people who would never have had an individual voice of influence.

This megaphone amplifies even the most minute of messages.

For example, if a video goes viral online, it can create a celebrity out of a "normal" person who might never have found fame otherwise.

Creating viral content such as videos, blog articles, motivational picture quotes and other content has become a mainstream marketing strategy which has put multi-billion dollar corporations and small businesses on equal footing. Rather than the size of the marketing budget dictating how many people are reached, it is the social proof that determines the reach.

Interestingly enough, people don't always have to "like" such content to produce this viral effect.

In 2013, Rebecca Black's parents bought her a birthday present many other 13 year old's probably only dream of. They paid for a song to be written for Rebecca, and recorded by her and filmed as a music video.

The music video for her song, "Friday," became the most hated YouTube video in history, quickly racing to 1,000,000 DISlike ratings on the video site as her video raced past 10,000,000 views. The more people watched the video, the more others wanted to watch it. People even "shared" the video on social media sites and encouraged other people to watch it to see how "awful" it was.

The result? One article reported that, now 16-year-old Rebecca, was earning $30,000 from YouTube ad-revenue shares and iTunes downloads.

All that being said, be careful with using this concept in this way. The old saying, "even bad press is good press," is not true when it comes to social proof. One negative report on a "rip off report" website can rank number one on search engines and create serious damage to a company's revenues.

Positive ways to create social proof for your business and other influence situations include:

- Creating "sharable" picture quotes for social media sites
- Asking for testimonials and referrals from your existing clients
- Highlighting situations where many other people have done what you want your subject to do

- Creating polls or petitions
- Gathering a crowd of like-minded people
- Showing, in any way, that others are "on board"

CHAPTER TWELVE

The Need for Consistency

We humans have a high need to appear consistent with commitments we make to others, whether verbal, in writing, or even implied. We just don't like to appear to be hypocrites.

For the most part (unless you're dealing with a sociopath), getting a verbal or written commitment to an outcome, will nearly insure that outcome from the person – especially if that person will have to face you again after making the commitment.

Numerous studies have been conducted to verify this, such as the one illustrated in Robert

Cialdini's groundbreaking book, *Influence.*

In the experiment, a researcher visited ten houses on one street of a neighborhood and asked each resident if they would be part of a campaign to promote "safe driving" in their neighborhood. Each resident was asked to sign a petition as a show of their commitment. All ten residents agreed and signed the petition.

Three months later, researchers returned to the neighborhood with an ugly 10' x 10' sign with the words, "Please Drive Safely," in paint on the front.

This time, they brought this sign down <u>two</u> streets. The original street which they had visited earlier with the petition, and another street they had not previously visited.

When they asked residents of the new, unvisited street if they would be willing to allow the sign in their front yard, only 20% of residents said, "yes," while 80% said, "No way!"

When they asked the residents of the previously visited street the same question, 80% of people said, "yes," while only 20% of residents said, "No way!" This was a stark difference in support.

When questioned how much they thought signing the petition had influenced their decision, none of the residents had even remembered the previous visit until they were asked about it.

This means the act of making a commitment influenced them subconsciously, even though they didn't consciously remember making it.

This shows the power of commitments.

Often, getting the sale is about more than just

getting a person from "no" to "yes". You must incrementally inch the prospect along the spectrum:

No ➔ Not Now ➔ Maybe ➔ Probably ➔ Yes

These incremental steps are called "micro-commitments," and I would say 99% of influence situations take this form, rather than just trying to get a "yes."

Many public speakers who sell high-ticket items from stage will try to get 200 or more "little yesses" before they make their pitch to the audience. Every little yes insures they will get a higher closing rate at the end of their talk.

CHAPTER THIRTEEN

RAPPORT AND LIKING

Dr. Robert Cialdini documented the power of Liking in the social psychology book, Influence. The fact is, people are much more likely to buy from you if they like you... but the question always arises, "How do I actually get people to like me?"

This is an age-old desire, but society seems to be split into those few who are "charismatic," and the rest of us who fumble awkwardly through that initial connection with another person.

It often seemed as though charisma is something that some are born with and others just don't have it, until the founders of NLP modeled one of the most charismatic people in the world, famed psychiatrist and hypnotherapist, Milton H. Erickson, who also brought us many of the influence patterns you've learned in this book.

Milton had a certain charm that was instantaneously felt in his presence. People could not put their finger on why they liked him.... They just did.

The roots of this technique go back to an amazing discovery made in the 1960s. Social psychologists wanted to find out if, like other animals, humans had a "mating dance."

So they decided to study humans who were about to mate in their native habitat: singles bars! They would sit in the corner with their notepads observing strangers (and possible mates), taking notes.

Ultimately, they failed to discover a human mating dance, but they did discover something amazing. When strangers would meet and begin to get into rapport (a sense of liking), their bodies and behaviors would begin to get into sync. They would laugh at the same time, shift in their seats at the same time, reach for their drinks at the same time, and if rapport developed, it was almost as if a "bubble" would envelop them and the rest of the world would "disappear."

Now, the body is what we call a psycho-cybernetic system, which means that the mind affects the body, and the body also affects the mind, like a cycle.

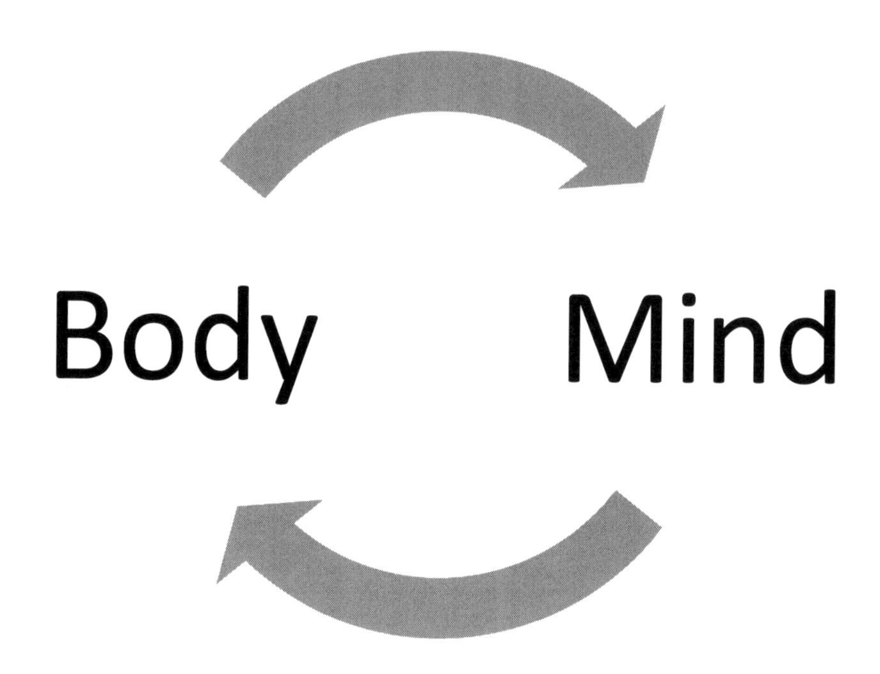

For example, being happy (mind) makes you smile (body), but it's also scientifically proven that smiling will make you happy.

So, if being in a state of rapport (mind) causes you to sync with the other person (body), then this "circuit" tells us that syncing with the other person will create rapport!

Rapport Sync

This is precisely what Milton Erickson was doing, which created a strong, instantaneous rapport and why people thought he was so charismatic.

To create rapport, begin by matching things you notice about the person. How are they standing or sitting? What is their posture? Is their head tilted or straight? Do they have a certain look on their face?

These are all physical characteristics of your subject that can be matched which will begin to create a sense of rapport automatically. It's like magic, and it happens completely out of the person's conscious awareness!

This was the "magical" quality that Milton Erickson had which allowed him to get his clients to do nearly *anything* for him, within moments of meeting him.

But beware: the point of matching the other person is to create <u>subconscious</u> rapport, not to catch their conscious attention and make them think you're mimicking them! Rapport is to be done <u>subtly</u>, so as to only tickle the subconscious mind.

Next, listen to their tone of voice. Is their

voice forceful or hushed? Is the pitch high or low? Rough or smooth? Loud or quiet? Are they speaking fast or slow?

Match the elements of their voice to gain subconscious rapport. The more rapport you have, the more people will feel that they know, like and trust you.

Finally, begin to listen to the words, ideas and expressions of the subject. They will be telling you about their state, and you had better match it if you want to have any measure of influence and persuasion.

Get Your FREE **Influence to Proft Resource Kit** with more great examples, influence scripts, bonuses, and videos at:

www.InfluenceToProfit.com/book-resource-kit

CHAPTER FOURTEEN

GOING FOR AGREEMENT

It has been said that when there's a disagreement, we don't listen to understand, we listen to reply.

There are several words which trigger this response more than others, and one of the most common is the word "but."

The word "but" is a word that negates everything that comes before it. Think about it... you probably wouldn't want someone to say, "You look good, but...," or "I'm sorry, but...," or even worse, "I love you, *but*..."

In a disagreement, it's often used in the form, "I understand, but...," which usually really means, "Shut up, I want to talk."

In sales, this usually sounds argumentative, breaks rapport and causes people to stop listening, so they can concoct their rebuttal.

So, as a general rule, avoid the word "but" and replace it with the word "and."

And is a word that conjoins two ideas. The human brain is designed to continue listening when it hears the word "and."

To maximize agreement, avoid the phrase, "I understand," and couple the word, "and," with the following phrases.

- "I agree, and..."
- "I appreciate that, and..."
- "I respect that, and..."

Here are some examples:

Prospect: "Your product is too expensive."
Ethical Influencer: "I appreciate that, and I'm sure you know the cost of buying something that is too cheap. You want the best quality, don't you?"

Prospect: "I'm not sure I trust you."
Ethical Influencer: "I respect that, and these testimonials from our clients show how valuable the product is to them."

Prospect: "This seems really complicated."
Ethical Influencer: "I agree, and after a few tries, you'll become a pro like all our other clients did."

Get Your FREE **Influence to Proft Resource Kit** with more great examples, influence scripts, bonuses, and videos at:

www.InfluenceToProfit.com/book-resource-kit

CHAPTER FIFTEEN

SALES CLOSING SECRETS

The "Close" is the part of sales that most people dread.

It's the moment where you ask for the money. It's do or die. If they say "no," it's over.

But there is hope. By modeling the best-of-the-best sales people, a task undertaken in the field of Neuro-Linguistic Programming, we can discover the "ninja" techniques that set the superstars apart from everyone else.

These sales-closing and objection-busting patterns were modeled from some of the top US Military recruiters in the nation.

These people have one of the toughest sales jobs in the world: Getting people to voluntarily give their life (figuratively and sometimes literally) up for their country.

If they can close the sale, you can, too, using the guerilla closes they use.

In the patterns listed on the following pages, "your outcome," represents the ultimate outcome you want from the client, i.e. buy your product.

1. Have you found that [your outcome] makes/gives you [benefit]?

This pattern allows you to covertly create a mental image of your outcome in their mind. It's a great assumption, because if they answer yes, they have agreed with you, and if they answer no, you can reply, "Oh, not yet?"

- Have you found that focusing on personal development makes you happier?
- Have you found that becoming a member of a strong team like ours makes you a better network marketer?
- Have you found that investing in something that you're obviously excited about motivates you in life?
- Have you found that when you really make a commitment to something you believe in, you find ways to cover the investment, even when you weren't sure you'd be able to?

2. Would it be fair to say [your outcome]?
This is another great pattern for building a mental image of your outcome. Most people are unwilling to call something "unfair," especially if it sounds reasonable or plausible.

- Would it be fair to say that buying this product will allow you more free time for your family and for yourself?
- Would it be fair to say that the more you consider your reasons for enrolling in this training, the less your excuses seem valid?
- Would it be fair to say that the more you think about how much you'll use this service, the easier it becomes to tell your friends and family about it?
- Would it be fair to say that taking the time to invest in this program is a small price to pay for [name one of their personal values]?

3. Just suppose...

These two words are the magic key to the treasure box of your prospect's imagination.

Based on the hypnotic "What If..." principle, these words direct your client to create a subconscious image of your outcome with far less critical judgment.

- I know you don't have the money right now, but just suppose you could come up with it. Where are some places it could come from?
- Just suppose you were to take this training. How can you see it changing your life?
- Just suppose you were to sign up today. Do you think your spouse would want to come too?
- Just suppose all of your objections were to melt away, you decided to make a down payment today, knowing that you'll find a way to cover the payments. When would you want to start now?

4. What would happen if [your outcome], because [their value]?

This very powerful pattern connects their value to your sale through the Cause→Effect persuasion pattern. Remember not to assume values for your client. Ask for them.

- What would happen if you purchased this service because you want to save money?
- What would happen if you enrolled in this training because you want to be closer to your family and to help your children?
- What would happen if you bought this product because you value smart investments?
- What would happen if you invested in yourself because you truly know that you're worth it?

5. Don't [action] unless you want [your outcome].

This is one of my favorite patterns, because the action and the outcome don't even have to be related, as long as the relationship sounds plausible. Because of the cause and effect relationship, if they find themselves doing the *action*, they will be subconsciously bound to *your outcome*. Because of that, the *action* can be either positive or negative.

- Don't even think about signing up for this training unless you really want to learn how to be successful.
- Don't sign this contract unless you're sure you want to make more money than you've ever made before.
- Don't even think about walking away unless you're absolutely positive that you're ready to make this profoundly positive change in your life.
- Don't even consider leaving your family at risk unless you're really committed to providing this for them now.

6. I appreciate [intent of their objection], and what would happen if [new behavior]? Because [reason]. And if you'd do that, I'd be willing to [concession]. This is a bigger language pattern, and it's a great objection obliterator!

- I appreciate that you want to save money, and what would happen if you enrolled in this program today? Because you know that in the long run, you'll not only make money, but save money. And if you'd do that, I'd be willing to waive the signup fee.
- I appreciate that your time is so precious, and what would happen if you enrolled in this training even though you didn't have the vacation time? Because these skills will certainly net you a raise, or even a promotion. And if you'd do that, I'd be willing to help you work to pitch it to your boss in his favor so that he might even approve paid time off.
- I appreciate that the risk of starting a new business is scary, and what would happen if you took those steps anyway? Because

you want the freedom of time to spend with your family, don't you? And if you'd purchase this business, I'd be willing to give you three months of coaching to help you get things rolling.

7. Yes, [negative feature objected to], and [positive feature of your proposal]. And if you're committed to [emotion/value], then you must be committed to [your outcome].

This is another powerful pattern combining the subconscious influence patterns of Complex Equivalence and Cause→Effect.

- Yes, our trainings are expensive, and they teach you to make more money right now. And if you're really committed to growing your business, then you must be committed to learning these techniques.
- Yes, our payment plan has a small monthly service fee, and the luxury of being able to pay over two years for benefits you'll

receive right now is the reason that makes sense. And if you're committed to achieving those goals you told me about, then you must be committed to getting started today, even if you need a little help.

- Yes, a few people have cancelled their subscriptions in the past, and they're missing out on the new benefits we've added that makes this service worth even more than your investment. And if you're really committed to protecting your family, then you must be committed to keeping them safe in the way that makes the most sense.

8. [Your outcome] and I appreciate [future obstacles]. Imagine for a moment that, together, we/you overcome [future obstacles], as we've/you've done in the past. Don't you feel good about that now?

This is a great pattern that helps to align past, present and future to a "Yes."

- I want to see you successful in this venture, and I appreciate that you're not sure about the economy in the next few months. Imagine for a moment that, together, we overcome that by making conservative investments that protect your savings, as we've done in the past. Don't you feel good about that now?
- I want to see you achieve that ideal body you've wanted for so long, and I appreciate that the holidays are coming. Imagine that we overcome those temptations by having you come in now, before the "holidays weight" gets put on,

as I've done with so many of my clients in the past. Don't you feel good about booking an appointment right now?

- I know you want the benefits of a security system, and I appreciate that you're worried about the monthly fees. Imagine for a moment that, together, we create an affordable payment plan for you, as we've done so many times in the past. Doesn't it make you feel good to know your family will be protected even when you're not home?

SUMMARY

Go Forth and Be Influential

Throughout this book, you're seeing new ways to speak to people. Ways of communicating that influence others like never before. As you watch the results you get from these techniques unfold, you'll find yourself becoming an Ethical Influencer.

You've been reading this book, page by page, chapter by chapter, learning many new things, and that means *you're growing*. I'm not going to suggest that this will be your favorite influence book of all time, but as you finish this book in its entirety, you're becoming more confident, more effective and more charismatic.

After you visit my website at **InfluenceToProfit.com/book-resource-kit** and discover all of the ways you'll learn to become a SUPER Influencer, you'll be practically unstoppable. It's your desire to *take my online courses* or live classes that will make you even more successful, or perhaps just that much more happy.

Ultimately, the best way to be persuasive is to always influence with integrity, speak from your heart, and seek win-win outcomes for everyone involved.

Years from now, when you're still getting results from learning this, perhaps you'll look back on it as a fond memory, or maybe you'll just really enjoy it. Either way, I know that the many friends you've recommended this book to will love you for it, now, don't they?

Go now, Ethical Influencer. Your destiny awaits!

PART TWO

Influence Language Pattern Reference

The following pages contain a reference of language patterns that bypass the critical conscious mind and have a definite effect on the subconscious mind.

I suggest you practice each language pattern individually, rather than trying to newly use all of them at once. For example, pick one pattern per day and just practice that pattern.

For more information on learning and using these patterns, be sure to check out our **Influence To Profit** live three-day training at www.InfluenceToProfitLive.com.

PATTERN ONE

Mind Reading

Claiming to know the thoughts or feelings of another person without saying how you knew, as if you were reading their mind.

Examples:

- I know you're wondering. . .
- I know you believe. . . .
- I know you came here for a purpose.
- I know how you like that.
- I know that you knew that.
- I know that you're in a nice trance now.
- I know that you're learning a lot here today.
- I know that tomorrow you will learn even more than today.
- I know that when you leave this training, you will be much wiser.
- I know you all studied very hard before you came here.

- We know you don't care.
- I knew you were thinking that.
- I'm sure you're aware. . .
- I'm sure you felt. . .
- You probably are aware. . .
- You probably also know
- I bet you're upset about that.
- I realize you already know. . .
- I can tell you're happy.
- I can tell how you feel. . .
- I can tell you've had a trying day.
- I can see you believe. . .
- I see that you know. . .
- You are enjoying Michael's book right now.
- I feel that you're learning a lot here today.
- I know that when you finish this book, you will be much wiser
- I know that you will learn even more at the live event.
- It's clear that you want to, don't you?
- We can tell you care.

PATTERN TWO

VALUE JUDGEMENT

Sharing a value judgment on someone or something, but not saying who is did the judging.

- It's bad to…
- That's good.
- That's right.
- That's too bad.
- It's good when…
- That's perfect!
- It is important to. . .
- It's wrong to cheat.
- Today is a great day!
- It's best to do sales with integrity.
- It's good to study hard.
- It's important to learn.
- It's good to dispute that
- It's great to always be right!
- It's great that you can change.
- It's really good that you say that.
- It's better to give than to receive.

- It was not right of you to say that.
- You're wrong.
- And it's awesome to wonder
- It's great to learn to influence at the live training.

PATTERN THREE

Cause and Effect

Implying that one thing causes or caused another. It's not necessary for it to be true for it to be accepted… it's only necessary for it to sound plausible.

Note, in some of these sentences, the words "then you" is simply replaced with a comma.

- If I help you, then you'll learn this.
- As you sit there, then you can feel wonderful.
- Don't think of taking this home, unless you want to make more money.
- Don't sit there unless you want to see something amazing.
- As you listen closely, you will learn faster.
- As you think about confidence then you can feel more confident.

- Reading this sentence, you get better and better.
- You can hear the music helping you to relax now
- Just your being here makes you want to learn this.
- As you ask that question, then you begin to understand.
- Because we are here, you are learning many new things
- As you sit here and listen to this, you are learning so much.
- Because you are here, you are going to learn NLP more easily.
- You will become more relaxed as you feel the fresh air coming in.
- As you contemplate these patterns, you can understand this deeply…
- And that's because they're artfully vague.
- Reading Michael's book makes you want to take his training.

PATTERN FOUR

COMPLEX EQUALITY

Referring to two things as being equal, or their meanings being equal. Again, it is not necessary for the equivalence to be true for the person to accept the statement. It is necessary for it to sound plausible.

- You are relaxing, and that means you're feeling good now.
- Being here means that you will change.
- Your question means you know it already.
- Asking questions means you are learning.
- Going to bed early means you will be alert.
- Knowing the answer means you are competent.
- Regular exercise means you are a better athlete.
- Your being in this group means your understanding will deepen.

- Being here <u>means</u> you will enjoy the process.
- Breathing that way <u>means</u> you'll relax even more
- Sitting in this room <u>is</u> an indication that you are learning many things.
- The fact that you want to learn <u>means</u> that you will.
- Just getting here <u>means</u> that you're willing to change.
- You'll soon <u>be</u> a better influencer.
- Michael <u>is</u> a good teacher.
- Regularly exercise <u>means</u> you will get healthy.
- You've come a long way, and that <u>means</u> that you're ready to buy.
- Listening closely <u>means</u> you're learning wonderful things.
- Michael's book <u>is</u> the best book.
- And that <u>means</u> you'll attend his live training.

PATTERN FIVE

PRESUPPOSITIONS

Using language that assumes an outcome; assumptive language.

- When you take this home, you'll see how powerful it is.
  (Assumes they will take it home. When, not if)
- How else could you get this much value from a product?
  (Assumes they will get value from the product)
- You can see the benefits more clearly now.
  (Assumes they see benefits)
- You'll be able to get even more tomorrow.
  (Assumes they will get some today)
- After you finish this book, the live course is even better.
  (Assumes you will finish the book AND attend the training)

- You can go through this process even more quickly
  (Assumes they will/have gone through the process)
- Which kind of benefit do you want today?
  (Assumes they want benefits)
- You realize you have more choices than ever before.
  (Assumes they have choices)
- You can easily move in the direction of your goals.
  (Assumes they have goals. Assumes they can move toward them)

PATTERN SIX

UNIVERSAL GENERALIZATIONS

Generalized statements that apply to everything or nothing (no in-between). "Black and white" statements fit in this category.

- Nobody's perfect.
- Everything you know helps you make this decision.
- All the things you like about this product are true.
- Everyone's buying this model.
- So every time you think of this conversation, you'll know you made the right choice.
- All the feelings there are to feel make you feel wonderful
- With everything that's happening in the world, you need this more than ever.
- Everything is wonderful.
- We are all in agreement.

- There is always today.
- Everyone knows it to be true.
- There is always more to learn.
- Everybody knows buying something new and shiny is easy.
- One can never know all there is to know.
- Everything in this room enhances your satisfaction.
- You can benefit from everything we're doing here today.
- Every part of this book makes everyone want to take all of Michael's trainings.

PATTERN SEVEN

POSSIBILITY/NECESSITY

Words of possibility or necessity. These words are important in influencing people because ever since we learned to talk the "rules" in life have been communicated through these words (can/can't, should/shouldn't, must/mustn't, will/won't, etc.)

- You should care about your family's safety.
- You should clearly see the value in this product now.
- You could take it home today and see how you like it.
- You must be aware of the benefits of this model.
- You may discover this is your favorite product of them all.
- You simply can't leave until you've tried this.
- You might be wondering about how I'm going to make this affordable.

- You may not like what the competition is doing.
- It's possible to have your cake and eat it, too.
- You may find, the more you read this book, that you could see yourself going to the live training. And you should, because you can.

PATTERN EIGHT

FROZEN VERBS

Verbs or processes that have been "frozen" in time by turning them into nouns. To test a noun to see if it is a frozen verb, ask, "Can I put it in a wheelbarrow?" If the answer is no, it is a nominalization.

Examples:

Verb	Frozen Verb (Noun)
act	actions
think	thoughts
emote	emotions
state	statements
object	objections
feel	feelings
to speak	a speech
to run	a run
learn	learnings

- This will provide you with new insights,

and new understandings about your desire for these benefits which you know you want.

- Your statements won't fall on deaf ears.
- You know my feelings on this subject.
- With all the learnings you have received from this reading, you'll have to release all controls over your motivations to attend the live training.

PATTERN NINE

VAGUE ACTIONS

Verbs (action words) that don't specify which action taken.

- Just do it.
- Act now, while there's still time.
- Just let go.
- You may continue.
- Go on.
- After you're done doing this, you can go.

PATTERN TEN

TAG QUESTIONS

- ...isn't it?
- ...have you?
- ...will you?
- ...won't you?
- ...haven't you?
- ...aren't we?
- ...aren't you?
- ...don't you now?
- ...don't you think?
- ...won't you, now?
- ...couldn't you . . .?
- ...wouldn't you now?
- ...can you not?
- You want to attend Michael's training, don't you?

PATTERN ELEVEN

Unspecified Subject

A sentence where the subject (the person/thing being talked about) is left out, or is not a specific person or thing.

Because the subconscious mind takes everything personally, it will often step into the role of the unspecified subject and accept the suggestion in the sentence as being about itself.

- One can decide easily, you know...
- People do all the time.
- They're watching us.
- It's weighing heavy on their shoulders.
- It is, you see.
- That's the way.
- People can learn
- Now you've got it!
- One can easily see
- You know the feeling.
- You may or may not know it.
- You can just let it go now.

- A person can easily take it home.
- I have something that will help you be more comfortable.
- Do you see things more clearly, now?
- One can accomplish all kinds of things.
- When you can notice that certain thing
- People come to Michael's training to learn how to do that.

PATTERN TWELVE

VAGUE COMPARISONS

- You're even more relaxed.
- You will enjoy this more.
- You're doing better now.
- The finer things in life.
- But that's neither here nor there.
- In a moment, you're going to be more intrigued...
- But it's better to get it now before it's too late.
- That's a nicer thought.
- We're #2, so we try harder.
- We are less expensive.
- We are more affordable.
- Michael's live trainings are better and higher quality which means you'll influence faster and more naturally.

PATTERN THIRTEEN

PACING CURRENT EXPERIENCE

Using words which match (also known as pace) the person's current experience in the moment. This is useful to repeat three times in succession, creating a "yes set." The most important thing is to remark on things which are undeniably true, which the person cannot contradict.

This builds rapport and makes it easier for the person to accept what you are about to say.

- You're here at the dealership, talking with me, and looking for a car that is just the right fit for your family, and that's why I believe this is the right car for you.
- You've done your research, looked at the brochure, and gotten approval from

your wife, so we can now move forward and finalize the paperwork.

- You're sitting there, looking at me, listening to the sound of my voice, and that means you're ready to do this now, aren't you?
- You've read this book, and learned new things, and become more influential, and that's why going to Michael's event is the right thing to do next.

PATTERN FOURTEEN

DOUBLE BINDS

Offering two choices which both lead to the same outcome.

- Would you like to book an appointment on Tuesday or Thursday?
- Would you like to take three or five of these home today?
- Will that be cash or credit?
- Do you want to do that here or before you leave?
- Would you like to just buy the car now, or test drive it before you buy it?
- Would you rather do that before or after your meeting?
- Would you like to go to bed at 8:45, or at a quarter till nine?
- Would you like to attend Michael's live event in the US or the UK?

PATTERN FIFTEEN

QUESTIONS

Commands which have been disguised as a question, making them more acceptable.

- Can you imagine this new car in your garage?
- Can you close the door?
- Will you sign this document?
- Could you picture how happy your wife will be?
- Can you see what I'm saying?
- Can you reach that level now?
- Would it be alright to feel this good about buying it today?
- Do you know that you know it already?
- Could you open your mind for a moment?
- How easily do you think you can do this?
- Can you remember to be kind to yourself?
- Does this sound like it will work for you?

- Do you feel prepared to sign the contract now?
- Do you think you want to take it home right now?
- Would you like to sign the paperwork now?
- Wouldn't you like to just complete this and move on?
- Is it ok for a person to have the amount of fun you'll have at Michael's live event?

PATTERN SIXTEEN

EXTENDED QUOTES

- The other day, I was talking to Joe in shipping who told me that the delivery guy, Jorge, was making a delivery to the CEO of Jones and Smith and he said ours is the best product on the market.
- CNN reported on Thursday that Warren Buffet has made his recommendation based on a talk he had with Bill Gates who's wife uses our product every day.
- The ADA says that three out of five dentists report that their patients like the taste of Listerine.
- Patty came to Michael's training because Mark told her that Michael's are the best. At least that's what Joe told him.

PATTERN SEVENTEEN

PERSONIFICATION

Personifying inanimate things bypasses the logical mind (a talking train, for instance, does not make sense, consciously) to engage the subconscious mind on the level of imagination.

- This product really wants you to take her home.
- What is your heart telling you to do?
- Imagine the story these walls could tell...
- "The little engine that could"
- My feet are screaming at me!
- My car knows which way to go.
- That plaid suit screams, "used car salesman!" (no offense to used-car salesmen!)
- Michael's trainings are reeling me in like a fish on a hook!
- This book is really encouraging you to go to the live training, it's it?

PATTERN EIGHTEEN

UTILIZATION

Using whatever communication, the person gives you in a constructive way without ever disagreeing. Verbal aikido.

- **Person:** "I don't know."
  Ethical Influencer: "I know you don't know. But if you did know, what would the answer be?"

- **Person:** "I can't be influenced."
  Ethical Influencer: "You're right, you can't be influenced *yet*."

- **Prospect:** "I'm not sold."
  Ethical Influencer: "That's right, because you haven't asked the one question yet that will let you be totally and completely sold now."

- **Person:** "I'm not convinced."
  Ethical Influencer: "Of course you're not convinced yet, because I haven't told you the best part."

- **Prospect:** "I have to talk to my wife."
  Ethical Influencer: "You most certainly do have to talk to her. She needs convincing. And the best way to do that is to take it home and show her how valuable it is... otherwise she won't believe you."

ABOUT THE AUTHOR

MASTER NLP TRAINER
AND BUSINESS COACH

MICHAEL STEVENSON

Michael Stevenson is a Master Trainer of Neuro-Linguistic Programming, the study of the mind and how language affects it.

He's a best-selling author of more than 10 books, an international speaker and a highly-successful business coach and consultant.

Michael is the co-owner of Influence to Profit (www.InfluenceToProfit.com) with his wife Kayla. Influence to Profit teaches business owners, marketers and sales professionals how to make more money with less resistance using ethical influence and persuasion through Michael's online courses and live events. If you're looking to learn more, the **Secrets of**

Subconscious Influence Home Study or the **Influence to Profit Live Training** are your next step.

To work with our team personally to take your business and/or marketing to the next level, consider joining **Thrive Program** coaching, education, and mastermind program. You can read more about this VIP coaching program at www.InfluenceToProfit.com/thrive-program.